OLD CAERPHILLY & DISTRICT
IN PHOTOGRAPHS

1 (*Overleaf*) The Twyn, *c*.1897, with the brook in front of the castle on the left and 'Pegleg' Fullalove standing on Doctor's Hill. The large house in the centre was occupied by Dr Llewellyn. The *Boar's Head* is on the right

Old Caerphilly

& District in photographs

by

Howard C. Jones

Foreword by Sir Trevor Evans, C.B.E.

STEWART WILLIAMS

Barry

First published March, 1979
Second impression September, 1979

© Stewart Williams, Publishers,
Bryn Awel, Buttrills Road,
Barry, South Glamorgan

To my wife Hazel

ISBN 0 900807 32 6

Printed in Wales by D. Brown & Sons Ltd., Cowbridge and Bridgend

Foreword

by Sir Trevor Evans, C.B.E.

NOSTALGIA is a powerful emotion. Whenever Abertridwr, Senghenydd, Caerphilly or Llanbradach are mentioned in my presence I am carried off on a magic carpet of the happiness of growing up. Fate could not have chosen a more comforting location.

No comparably compact area in the world, I boast, could have lived through, within a decade, the grief of the Senghenydd disaster of October 1913, when 439 men, relatives, neighbours and friends were killed with all the cataclysmic consequences on their families —and the ecstatic fervour of the religious revival of 1922, with such universally shared emotions. And there was the Great War in between, when we all subscribed to a 'Welcome Home' Fund, and every man who came home 'on leave' in uniform was given a pound if from a Fighting Front and ten shillings if from Training Camp. That spending money was appreciated in those days.

Of course, each village had its local pride, like the Silver Band and the Children's Choir in Abertridwr and a useful Rugby club in Senghenydd, but we rarely came to blows, except sometimes on Saturday mornings when the youngsters from the two villages had a bit of a scuffle in the lane behind the Welsh Church conveniently located on the Senghenydd side of 'the divide'.

Llanbradach was slightly isolated—but for two factors. On the morning of 'the explosion' the miners of Llanbradach were the first to come over the mountain trail into Cwmceffyl to offer their services as rescue workers, and this was remembered for years. Secondly, when the youngsters of Abertridwr climbed that trail in reverse there, fairly precipitously below, was Llanbradach, the key not only to the Rhymney Valley but to England and the East. Few Llanbradach folk could ever have imagined that to some they were the outer portals of the Gateway to London!

Caerphilly was our 'Big Brother'—and for so many reasons. The Council Offices were there. And so was the Police Court. The shops in those days offered a wider range than in most valley villages; but most of all, there was Caerphilly railway station, which some thought of as a miniature Clapham Junction. It actually had seven platforms. From the valleys you had to go through Caerphilly, and you changed for everywhere else, except Cardiff. You changed for Newport, you changed for Pontypridd, you changed for Bargoed and the Rhymney Valley—that's when there were trains, of course.

And every Easter Caerphilly held its Baptist Cymanfa Ganu in Tonyfelin when all the Baptist chapels from miles around had one predominant ambition—to out-sing the interdenominational Gymanfas held every Christmas alternately in Senghenydd and Abertridwr. I think the latter won because they would hold full-scale rehearsals for a month before 'The Day'.

I suspect, however, that what welded the homogeneity of the valley villages were the surrounding hills, and the wooded glades between them. They were—and are—beautiful and permanent; over the top above Senghenydd to restful Llanfabon, to benign Eglwysilan on the path to Pontypridd; around Mynydd Meio, for a stimulating view of the

Taff Valley to Groeswen and back over the fields to Abertridwr; and there are few more exciting views, after coming over the top of the road to Caerphilly from Cardiff after dusk, than the twinkling lights of the valleys below.

Maybe because Nature's surrounding casket is so fair, its contents—the townships and their inhabitants—are blessed with many worthy attributes, such as stoicism in calamity and enthusiasm in exaltation. The memory of such attributes—I left Abertridwr 54 years ago—remains excitingly verdant.

Trevor Evans

Introduction

A CENTURY ago, Caerphilly was a little market town, Llanbradach simply the name of a couple of farms and the Aber Valley an unspoiled rural backwater of fields and woodland. A few of the pictures in this book give a glimpse of this period, for example the one showing the railway being built through Abertridwr and others illustrating thatched cottages at the *Bowls Inn* and the Warren. It is true industry was present, but only on a relatively small scale, at the Rhos Llantwit Colliery, Caerphilly, at the corn mills and woollen mills and at Pwllypant Quarry, for instance. But the area was still predominantly an agricultural one.

In the 1890s, however, the sinking of the deep collieries at Llanbradach, Senghenydd and Abertridwr changed all that. The landscape was transformed and thousands of men, women and children flocked in to make turbulent new communities around the collieries. Pictures have survived from this period and I was thrilled to discover two photographs of the men who actually carried out the sinking of the Universal Colliery, Senghenydd. Caerphilly also underwent great changes at the turn of the century. In the 1880s, an American visitor described it as 'an unattractive place, where poverty suns itself on the doorstep... untidy children, with miserable, pinched faces, roll in the paths or sprawl in the open doors of shops and beer houses'. That was the time when Caerphilly was little more than a village strung between Piccadilly and the Twyn. By 1900, however, much had been rebuilt and Cardiff Road was developing as a second shopping street to Castle Street. Many terraces were being erected behind Cardiff Road and on the main roads leading away from the old centre. Several pictures in the first part of this book show the town as it then was, and how it was changing. While collieries were being opened around Caerphilly, on the town's outskirts the Rhymney Railway's locomotive repair sheds were opened in 1901 and became a major employer. Before the age of the motor car, Caerphilly was also a busy railway junction, with lines radiating in six different directions. But the horse and cart were to stay for many a year yet.

Pictures of streets, collieries and railways only give us a clue as to Old Caerphilly and District, however. If the times were characterised by harsh working conditions, low wages and poor housing, let us not forget that throughout Caerphilly, Llanbradach and the Aber Valley there was a thirst for the better things of life in religious, educational, cultural, social, political and sporting pursuits. Chapels and churches were not just for Sunday services. They had choirs, bands, drama groups, concert parties and some even had football teams— all aspects being illustrated in this book. In the early part of the century, the Aber Valley was still predominantly Welsh-speaking and many activities were carried out in the old language. Mrs Ann Jones, a grand old lady who died in Abertridwr in 1912 was a Welsh-speaker who never learned English, though she was kind-hearted enough to take in a Cockney family of lodgers. Caerphilly itself was already English-speaking, though there was a pocket of Welshness on Caerphilly Mountain and, of course, the town supported several Welsh chapels. The town had an annual eisteddfod every Whit Monday, though regrettably by 1889 it was a largely English eisteddfod. The district had a surprising number of self-help ventures, such as the Senghenydd and Aber Valley Co-operative Society, founded in 1897, several building clubs that built blocks of terrace housing and friendly societies such as the Oddfellows. Occasionally there were events to celebrate such as Queen Victoria's Diamond Jubilee, the Relief of Mafeking and the Royal Visit of 1907—all featured in this collection.

So far as visitors were concerned, Caerphilly was the home of the Castle and Caerphilly Cheese. Few came without seeing the fortress and few left without a piece of the cheese. Whatever the fame of Caerphilly, it was nothing to compare with the way the name of Senghenydd became known world-wide in 1913. The United Kingdom's worst colliery disaster left 439 dead, with 205 women widowed and 542 children fatherless, and this in a village that had lost 81 men in a colliery explosion only 12 years before. Four of the pictures reproduced here were part of the tasteless commercial exploitation of the disaster by the manufacturers of souvenir postcards, china-ware and trinkets.

I wonder who the teacher was who, with an ironic touch, decided that the children of miners in Senghenydd in 1899 should blacken their faces just like their fathers and dress up as 'Nigger Minstrels' in a school concert? This is just one of the many fascinating school photographs preserved in the district and reproduced in the section of religion and education. Many have been loaned by individuals but I must mention my stroke of luck in that two albums of school photographs were found in an attic during 1978 and handed to St Martin's Comprehensive School. School photographers have been visiting local schools as long ago as 1875. Look at the way the children's dress changed over the years, how the school furniture was modernised and how school activities varied. Many people will spot familiar faces, if not themselves or their parents. Here and there is a well-known name, such as Maudie Edwards, a star of *Welsh Rarebit*.

A section of the book is devoted to types of housing. The pictures of the Van Mansion show how it has deteriorated in the last 80 years. Lesser mansions have disappeared or are now almost unrecognisable. Gone too are The Huts, a long tin shed that housed several families in Senghenydd. A section on personalities includes the last squire of Ystrad House, some Caerphilly businessmen, Llanbradach and Abertridwr notables and some committees that played an important role in public life.

The final section on the Castle is closely linked with the first section on the town centre. For in the 1930s, the Marquess of Bute tore the heart out of the old town by demolishing one side of Castle Street and part of Cardiff Road. He wanted the Castle to be shown to better advantage and to prepare for the restoration of the water defences. This wholesale destruction, together with the demolition of the Twyn buildings, swept away a whole variety of shops, houses, a chapel and many business premises, including some public houses.

Much of the town's character disappeared, but fortunately we have a pictorial record of scenes that only the older generation can now recall.

My collection of pictures would not have been possible without the public-spiritedness of more than 40 people who have loaned items for inclusion, in addition to those made available by Cardiff Central Library, the Local History section of Mid Glamorgan County Library and by the Caerphilly branch library. Many people fail to appreciate the value of old photographs and postcards and they are destroyed. It is certain there are many items of historic interest remaining in private hands, perhaps stored in attics or drawers. I appeal to people who know of such items to make them available to a public library or to Caerphilly Local History Society, which has begun a collection with the hope ultimately that such photographs can form a strong basis for a Caerphilly Museum.

In addition to those people who have loaned photographs and who are listed at the end of the book, I would like to thank Sir Trevor Evans, C.B.E. for kindly providing a Foreword. I must, of course, acknowledge my debt to County Councillor H. P. Richards's book *A History of Caerphilly*, and to Mr Glyndwr G. Jones's series of *Cronicl Caerffili*. Both works are indispensible to those who wish to learn about Caerphilly's past, and both are by dedicated amateur local historians. I should also like to thank Mr Roger Padfield, of Cardiff Central Library, Mr David Pearce, of Mid Glamorgan County Library and Mrs Lindsay Williams, of Caerphilly branch library, for their help, Mr C. J. Taylor and Mr E. R. Mountford for specialist advice on transport, Mr Hubert Gatehouse and Mr Victor C. Hardacre for permission to use copyright photographs, and Mr Stewart Williams for making the whole thing possible. Finally I wish to thank my wife Hazel for her support and encouragement and my sons Philip and Robyn who patiently came on many trips to seek out old photographs that should prove as interesting to their generation as I hope they are to mine.

HOWARD C. JONES

20 St Ilan's Way,
Watford Farm Estate,
Caerphilly

The Town

2   The Market Hall next to the Twyn Chapel. Built in 1889, it was the cheese market until 1910 but survived
until the 1950s as a dance hall and furniture store

3/4 The Twyn, *c.*1936. Harris's corn store, the last building on the site of the present car park, was demolished *c.*1953

5 Markets of all kinds were held on the Twyn. This horse fair was held *c.*1907

6 The Twyn Chapel with original tower, *c.*1897. It ceased to be a chapel in 1963 and became a community centre in 1974

7 The Twyn from Castle Street, c.1897. The Cenotaph stands where the saddlers shop stood then

8/9 Castle Street in the early 1900s (*above*) and *c.*1897. Nearly all the North side was demolished in the 1930s

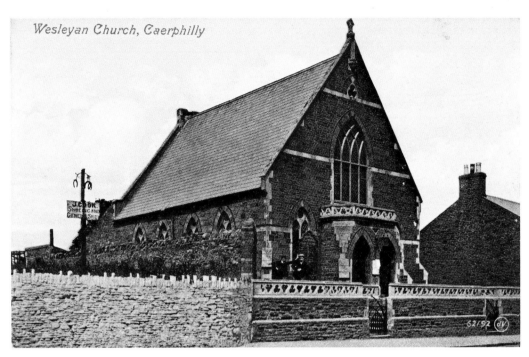

10 Wesley Chapel, Castle Street, built 1865, closed 1929. The horse-shoes advertised a smithy

11 The Cenotaph in the 1920s with the Castle Theatre on left and a furniture store on right

(*Opposite page*)

12 Castle Street before World War I

13/14 Castle Street during and after the demolition of the *Queen's Hotel* c.1935 The *Globe* is on the right

Castle St. Caerphilly. 76

15 Castle Street in 1930 before demolition work began

16 The former Castle woollen mill, built about 1800 and pulled down shortly after this 1936 picture. It stood in the dip below the present Co-operative Store

17 Piccadilly Square, *c*.1900. The corner house was removed in 1978

18 Pontygwindy Road, *c*.1900, from a postcard sold by E. A. Jones's post office next to where the little girl is standing

19/20 Cardiff Road in the 1890s (*above*) and about 1912 (*below*). Tesco now stands where the *Clive Arms* is shown on the right. The shops and cottages opposite were removed in the 1930s

21 The 18th-century *Clive Arms* demolished in 1894 with its last licensee, John Morgan, and his family

22 The Doctor's Hill in 1934, with a Western Welsh bus passing Candle King, a shop that sold cheap vegetables and dried fish for 2d. each

23 Cardiff Road, *c.*1897 when William Thomas of the *King's Arms* brewed his own beer and the cottages were rented for five shillings a week

24 Cardiff Road about ten years later than the previous picture

25 Lloyds Bank now stands where the cottages stood in the 1890s and Wildings occupies the corner shop. The horse was probably from an April fair

26 The oak tree outside St Martin's Church. Until its removal in 1913, local processions always marched around the tree before returning to town. A council chairman's chair was made from its timber

27 St Martin's Church shortly before the tower was added in 1910

28   Lon-y-llyn before the Beddau and Watford Fach fields were built on

29   The Old Bailey, near Piccadilly Square, demolished *c*.1936

Sport, Entertainment and Notable Events

30 Caerphilly Higher Elementary School's first soccer team with teacher Trafford Griffiths, 1914

31 Caerphilly Baptists soccer team with Beddau Farm behind, 1921

32 Caerphilly Baptists after their success in the Cardiff & District Sunday Schools League, 1929

33 Tredomen AFC, winners of Caerphilly Miners Hospital Cup, 1937. The captain, Frank Piper, won a Welsh amateur international cap in 1939

34 Pubs had football teams too, like this from the *Boar's Head* in the 1920s

35 Llanbradach Cricket Club *c*.1929, with Victor Hardacre on extreme left. He took many of the pictures in this book

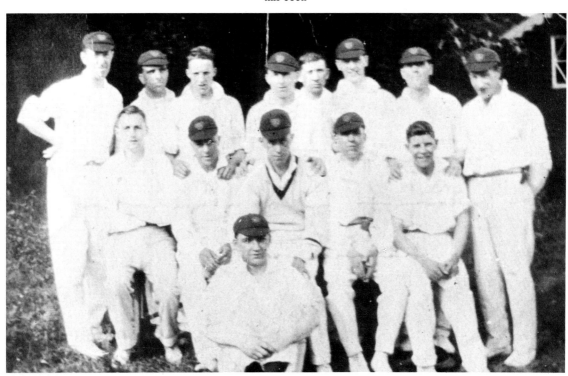

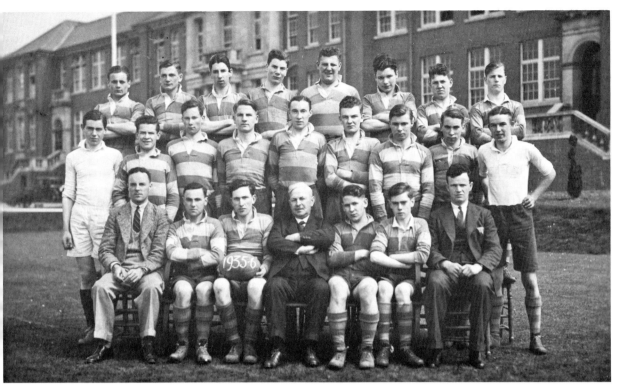

36 Caerphilly Boys' Secondary School rugby team, 1932, with headmaster W. Gladstone Rees (*centre*) and teachers Glyn Lloyd and Trevor Jenkins, later Glamorgan's director of education

37 Abertridwr Rugby Club in 1935

38/39 Hockey at the Caerphilly Higher Elementary School, 1914, with teachers Miss Rowlands and Miss Gertie Thomas, and Mount Carmel's tennis ladies in the 1930s

40/41 Keeping fit at Gwyndy Girls Secondary Modern School with teacher Mrs Eluned Thomas, 1947 and 1948

42 Caerphilly and District Choral Society, 1920

43 Llanbradach Ladies Choir, who won at the Rhyl National Eisteddfod, 1904, under conductress Mrs T. Moses

44 Caerphilly Male Voice Party who sang at the Park Hall, Cardiff, in June 1896

45 Abertridwr Children's Choir, conductor Ted Smith, *c*.1920

46 Gertrude Gronow, who lived in Caerphilly, with her Royal Welsh Ladies' Choir. They twice toured North America in the Twenties

47 Music in the streets the day after Mafeking was relieved in May, 1900. With the band in Cardiff Road is top-hatted the Rev. J. P. Davies, Tonyfelin

48 Van Road English Congregational Church band at the Old Oak, *c*.1909

49 Llanbradach Operatic Society present Joseph Parry's 'Blodwen' in 1928

50 A Communist Party supporter shows the flag alongside a Senghenydd procession of the 1920s

51 Mrs Mary Edwards was 100 years old on 16 May, 1950. Her chapel, Seion, Llanbradach, gave her a party and a place of honour at the top table

52 Shakespeare at Llanbradach during World War I

53 Drama at Beulah, Abertridwr, *c*.1912. The 'policeman' is Griffith Jones, the local librarian, whose son Arthur sits with hands clasped. Arthur Jones was an 'extra' in BBC TV's 'Off to Philadelphia in the Morning', in 1978

54 The Marquess of Bute entertained the Royal Archaeological Society at the castle in 1871, the 600th
anniversary of the fortress. They had a band to entertain them and a banquet in the Great Hall

55 King Edward VII and Queen Alexandra arrive at the castle on 13 July, 1907, via the old approach past the woollen mill

56 The Princess Royal at the castle in 1938 when the British Red Cross Society staged Macbeth, starring Donald Wolfit and a largely local cast. With the Princess is Sir Ewen Maclean and behind is the Marchioness of Bute

57 Sir Ifan ab Owen Edwards takes the salute during the Urdd National Eisteddfod at Caerphilly, 1933

58/59 The day war was declared in 1939, the 2nd Monmouthshire Regiment was in town and held a church parade. After the war, scores of street parties were held, like this one in Bridgefield Street, Abertridwr

60 Queen Victoria's Diamond Jubilee of 1897 was celebrated by local big-wigs with a function in the castle

61 The Caerphilly Eisteddfod Committee of 1896

62/63 Britain's worst mining disaster was at the Universal Colliery, Senghenydd, on 14 October, 1913, when
439 men and boys died. *Above*, a pithead scene, and *below*, a tired rescue party

Pit Disaster at Senghenydd. Heroes all. A rescue party leaving the Pit after an all night search.

64/65 *War Cry* carried this picture of the funeral of a Salvation Army member, Colour Sergeant E. Gibson. *Below*, the procession of coffins which went on for days

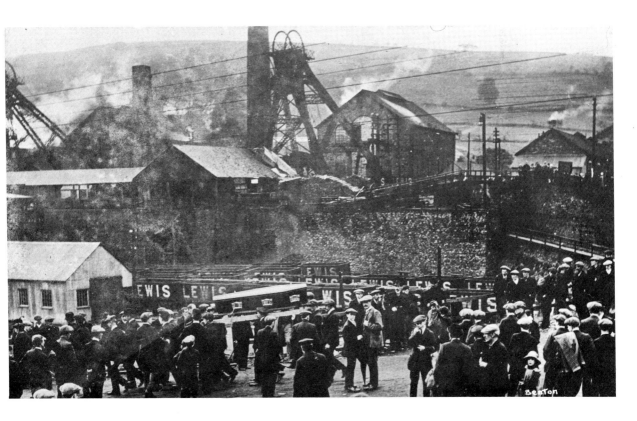

Transport

66 The hamlet that became Abertridwr. This 1893 picture shows the railway being built, cutting through the wooded slopes that later were covered by terraced houses and the Windsor Colliery's tips. The *Pandy Inn* and Abertridwr House can be seen clearly

67   The contractors' locomotive used in the building of the line to Senghenydd

68   Llanbradach Station, *c*.1900, with the colliery in its infancy, streets only partly built and the church without the tower

69 Caerphilly Station before the remodelling of 1913

70 Watford Crossing Cabin, with Jack Emmanuel holding a shovel, c.1912. This line was used for Pontypridd-Newport trains until 1956

71   A Rhymney Railway 'motor car' at Senghenydd, *c*.1908

72   Senghenydd Station, *c*.1919. Passenger trains ceased in 1964

73/74 The Rhymney Railway's locomotive work were opened in 1901 and became the town's chie employer after the collieries. *Opposite* is the 'walk ing crane' in the machine shop and *below* is th erecting shop, both in 1906

75/76 The boiler shop (*above*) and the wagon shop (*below*), both in 1906. The works, always known as 'The Sheds', were shut down in 1963 and were converted into the Harold Wilson Industrial Estate

77 Management, supervisory and clerical staff at 'The Sheds', 1932

78 Caerphilly U.D.C. became in 1920 the first South Wales authority to operate motor buses, beating Cardiff by eight months. This was one of the two Tilling Stevens solid-tyred petrol-electric buses

79 Caerphilly Chamber of Trade hired a Bristol Tramways charabanc for this late 1920s trip. Charles Goodfellow (president) and Percy Coleman (secretary) are up front

80 Roberts' fleet of Bedfords in 1943 carried headlamp masks and white bumpers for the blackout. Jess Roberts drove a bus for the council until he founded his business in 1928

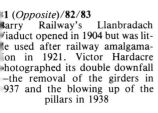

81 (*Opposite*)/**82/83**
Barry Railway's Llanbradach Viaduct opened in 1904 but was little used after railway amalgamation in 1921. Victor Hardacre photographed its double downfall —the removal of the girders in 1937 and the blowing up of the pillars in 1938

Religion and Education

84 Alderman J. E. Evans, a coal owner, with his Sunday School class at Mount Carmel English Baptist Church, Caerphilly, 1894

85 Mount Carmel's minister, the Rev. E. Roberts Lewis, (*standing, left*) with the 'Golden Star Brigade' in 1921

86 The Band of Hope of St Martin's Church, 21 April, 1904

87 The choirs of St Martin's and St Catherine's churches pose during their trip to Abergavenny and Raglan Castle, *c.*1905. The vicar is the Rev. Connop Price and one of the schoolboys is Percy Coleman

88 The girls who took part in a concert at Salem Welsh Baptist Chapel, Senghenydd, *c.*1905, would have heard very little English in this strictly all-Welsh chapel

89 A cantata called 'Princess Ju-Ju' at Abertridwr Welsh Congregational Chapel, *c.*1908

90 Ebeneser Welsh Baptist Chapel's minister, the Rev. D. M. Jones, was just at home canvassing for the Labour Party in Senghenydd as he was preaching in the pulpit

91 Dewi Wyn Watkins, christened at Abertridwr Chapel in 1948, now plays the cello for the Welsh National Opera

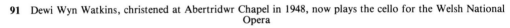

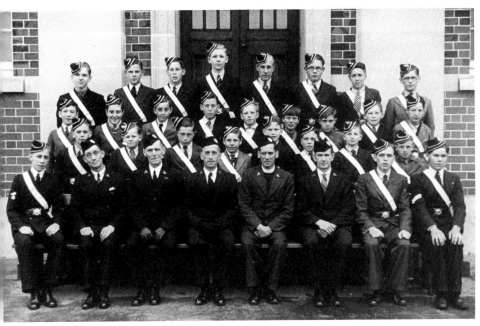

92/93 Mount Carmel Boys Brigade (*above*) and Sunday School members enjoying a treat at Plas Watford private swimming pool, *c*.1949

94 Caerphilly's annual Sunday School march, in Market Street, *c*.1949

95 Twyn schoolchildren shortly after E. M. Bevan (*right*) became headmaster in 1910

96 'Daughter of the Regiment' presented by Twyn children, *c*.1919. Violet Nicholls stands in the centre, and on her right is Maudie Edwards, later to become a famous radio comedienne and actress

97 Maudie Edwards (*seated*) also took part in 'Ali Baba'. The fairy is Miss Gwyneth Richards, who later became a local headmistress, and the turbanned sultan is Roy Howells

98 Top hats and tails at the Twyn, *c.*1919

99 Joseph Howells, buildings committee chairman, lays the foundation stone of the main Twyn Council School, 19 February, 1922

100 Twyn girls leaving for a trip to London with Miss Dora Brown

101 Twyn teachers in 1925. *Front:* Miss M Pierce, Mrs Katie Knight, Miss Dora Brown (head), Miss Annie Austin, Miss Annie Snell. *Back:* Miss Dorothy Napier, Miss Eleanor Miles (later Richards), Miss Mabel Griffin, Miss Betty Howells

102 Miss Annie Snell's class of 40 at the Twyn, 1925

103   Twyn Standard I with Miss Annie Austin, 1925

104   Twyn Standard IVB with Miss Mabel Griffin, 1925

105 Harry Simons's class at Caerphilly Boys' Secondary School, 1932. Mr Simons is now president of Caerphilly Local History Society

106 Physics at the Boys' Secondary School with Glyn Lloyd, who was secretary to the Caerphilly National Eisteddfod in 1952

107/108 Cookery for two generations, with smocks at the Caerphilly Higher Elementary School, 1914, and starched aprons and caps at the Gwyndy Girls' Secondary Modern, with Miss Betty Howells, 33 years later

109 Standard V at the Twyn Boys' School, 1927

110 Headmaster W. Gladstone Rees (*centre*) with his staff at the Boys' Secondary School, 1932

111   The orchestra at the Boys' Secondary School, 1932

112/113   Chemistry and physical education at the same school with teachers W. T. Griffiths and Trevor Jenkins

114 'Nigger Minstrels' at Senghenydd Junior School, 1900. The sight of a black-faced man would not have been unusual in this mining village!

115 Cwm Aber School pupils with the best attendance record, *c.*1918

116 Miss Edith Perret, who became a missionary in Africa, pictured with her class at the Girls' Secondary School in Crescent Road, *c.*1933

Trade and Industry

117 The steam bakery of M. Jones delivered to all districts. This picture was taken in the 1890s when Pentrebane Street was just cottages

118 Progress for Coleman Bros. bread carts meant changing cartwheels to pneumatic tyres, but keeping the horses

119/120/121 Manchester House looked like this (*opposite*) in 1900, being remodelled before 1912 (*below*). The shop staff of the 1920s are pictured above.

The Pharmacy, ✹ Caerphilly.

J. A. THOMAS, M.P.S.,

Family & Dispensing Chemist.

Special attention given to dispensing Physicians' and Surgeons'
——— Prescriptions. ———

THOMAS'S KURA KOF. ~ Per 1/~ Bottle.
SAFE.   CERTAIN.   SPEEDY.

A Sovereign Remedy for Bronchitis and all affections of the
. . . Throat and Lungs. . . .

OPTICAL DEPARTMENT.

Spectacles and Folders at all prices.   The Eyesight tested free
and defects of vision remedied and comfort ensured.

H. G. MABBETT,

PRACTICAL WATCHMAKER,
JEWELLER & OPTICIAN. . .

Has a Choice Selection of
Jewellery, Watches, Clocks, Electro & Silver Plate,
suitable for Wedding, Birthday and Complimentary Presents.

**Silver Souvenir Spoons.   Gold and Silver Souvenir
Brooches and Pendants.**

Spectacles to suit all sights. Oculists' Prescriptions
——— ——— skilfully made up. ——— ———
All Goods of superior quality at moderate prices.

REPAIRS. Any of the above articles cleaned and repaired on
the premises in best style at lowest charges consistent with good
workmanship.   All repairs guaranteed.

Gold Wedding, Engagement and Keeper Rings.

2, MARKET STREET, ✹ CAERPHILLY.
(In Centre of Town.)

124 Herbert Walters had a cafe on Senghenydd Square but took to the road to celebrate the Coronation in 1937. Can you spot the chicken?

125 Tom England (*right*) with his butcher shop, the last building to go in the demolition of Castle Street. It was removed after his death in 1948

ALL LOCAL
NO
IMPORTED

126 Tŷ Vaughan in the 19th century, now the site of Barclays Bank, an estate agents' and the Jobcentre

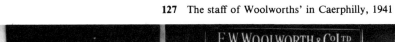

127 The staff of Woolworths' in Caerphilly, 1941

128 The *Bowls Inn*, when Margaret Price was the licensee in the 1890s

129 The *Royal Oak* on the Twyn, c.190? (*see* **1**). Licensee James Coggins was also a blacksmith and butcher. Mrs Eliza Coggins is seen with her granddaughter now Mrs Irene Bassett, and Harry Coggins

130 The *Black Cock Inn*, Caerphilly Mountain, *c.*1892, in the days when John Harris brewed his own beer there

131 *Aber Hotel,* Abertridwr, *c.*1900, with Powell's bread cart

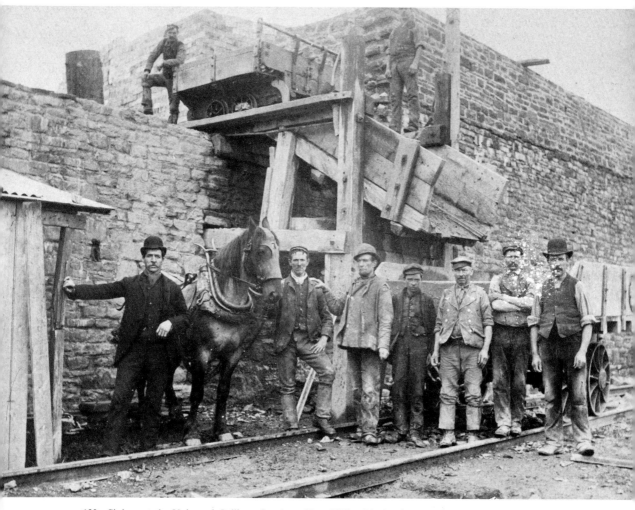

132 Sinkers at the Universal Colliery, Senghenydd, *c*.1892, with the chute used to load rubble directly on to trucks. The sinkers came mainly from the Mountain Ash area

133 Sinkers at the Universal Colliery beside temporary wooden pit gear

134 A farrier and other surface workers of the Rhos Llantwit Colliery, 1885. The colliery, whose site is now covered by part of Lansbury Park, Caerphilly, produced coal from 1864 to 1892

135 Rhos Llantwit colliers in the 1880s when they were producing 70,000 tons a year

136 The Coke Ovens at Llanbradach Colliery. Coal was first raised at Llanbradach in 1893 and at its peak it employed over 2,300. It closed in 1961

137 Senghenydd in about 1894 with the Universal Colliery nearing completion but the village only half-built

138 The same area shortly before the colliery shut in 1928, showing the 1904 police station and the other houses

139　The Universal Colliery between the two explosions. Eighty-one died in the 1901 accident, and 439 in 1913

140　Universal safety men and officials in 1920s with Colliery Sergeant James

THE WINDSOR COLLIERY,   ABERTRIDWR.   1872.

141   Windsor Colliery, opened in 1898, supplied the Royal Navy and other shipping with excellent steam coal, and in the 1920s employed over 1,600 men. It has been worked from Nantgarw since 1977

142   Windsor safety men during a strike in the 1920s

WINDSOR COLLIERY
ABERTRIDWR

143 Officials and safety men at the Windsor Colliery, *c.*1921

144 The quarry at Pwllypant supplied stone for Cardiff's later docks, many public buildings and churches such as St Martin's, Caerphilly

Llanbradach Quarry.   M.J.R.B. 8658.

145 Aber Corn Mill about the time it stopped working in the 1880s. The iron wheel can just be seen. Aber Mill School, opened in 1871, is on the hill

146 Frederick Morgan, last miller of Energlyn Mill, before it closed c.1910. Only one wheel is working but the negative has been doctored to give a water effect. The site is now occupied by Kenlea, Mill Road

Public Services

147 Tar-spreaders on the Ystrad Mynach road in 1914 included women and (*second from left*) a man called Peg-leg Goule

148 Senghenydd Town Guard in 1914 with Colliery Sergeant James, instructor

149 Percy Coleman (*right*) was the captain of Caerphilly's first fire brigade in the 1920s

150 Caerphilly detachment of the St John Ambulance Brigade *c.*1911, with Officer-in-charge G. H. Rigsby

151/152　Senior staff at Bronrhiw Red Cross Hospital in World War I (*from left*): Miss Enid Thomas, Miss Sybil Corbett, Miss Daisy Goodfellow and Mrs Savours. *Below*: Llanbradach Red Cross, *c*.1911

153 Dr Edward Savage and Col. D. J. Davies with Caerphilly members of the British Red Cross Society in the 1930s

154 Caerphilly Post Office in Cardiff Road before the present Post Office was opened in 1937. The building is now occupied by the Abbey National Building Society

155 Pwllypant crossroads in the 1930s. A Post Office occupies the old tollgate house on the corner

156 Caerphilly Urban District Council and staff, *c.*1929. William Spickett, clerk, is fourth from left in front row, and T. F. Owen, who became the first full-time solicitor-clerk, is third in back row

157 Groeswen Home Guard Patrol near Hendredenny, *c.*1943. *From left:* Pascoe Pardoe, of Hendredenny Hall, his son Jim and P. Phillips, of Garth Farm. This was the first such patrol in Glamorgan

158 Soup kitchen volunteers at Senghenydd in the 1920s

159 Caerphilly District Miners' Hospital opened with 12 beds on 30 June, 1923. This picture taken the same day shows Matron M. Thomas flanked by County Councillor J. Phillips (*right*) the chairman, and Henry Richards, secretary. Will Crews, later South Wales miners' secretary, is first in back row

Housing

160 Van Mansion, stately home in the 16th and 17th centuries of the Lewises, ancestors of the Earls of Pembroke, before they abandoned it for St Fagans Castle. The part on the left has collapsed since this picture was taken *c.*1900 and the rest is now in danger of falling

161 The Dovecote at the Van collapsed after the severe winter of 1947

162 Only a few walls now remain of these houses at the Van which were inhabited when this picture was taken
in the 1890s

163 Llanbradach Fawr in 1893. This part-Tudor farmhouse was the home of the distinguished Thomas family and gave its name to the colliery village

164 Pwllypant House a century ago, after it was bequeathed to the enormously rich Marquess of Bute by its eccentric squire, William Evans Williams, who hardly knew him. Bute's agent, J. S. Corbett, moved in and it is now *Corbett's Hotel*

165 Abertridwr House, the oldest building in the village until it was demolished in 1972

166 Pontypandy House, home of the wealthy Price family of entrepreneurs in the 18th century, was nearing collapse when this picture was taken, *c.*1948. Pontypandy Farm can be seen on the left

167 Porset Toll-gate House with Mrs Anne Thomas, who lived there from 1892 until she died in 1959. It stood next to Porset bridge on the old road between Caerphilly and Bedwas, and is mentioned in George Borrow's *Wild Wales*

168 Warren Cottages when they were still thatched, *c*.1913

169 The Huts, Senghenydd, in 1913. Built for colliery sinkers *c*.1891, they were occupied until 1928

170 An old lodging house near Bryncennydd, Nantgarw Road, Caerphilly, *c*.1930

171 Tinkers camped on the Rhos, near Pwllypant, a picture taken by a member of the Corbett family of
Pwllypant

Personalities

172 Lt. Col. H. E. Morgan Lindsay (1857-1935), colonel of the Royal Monmouthshire Engineers, Commander of the Bath, chairman of Caerphilly U.D.C. in 1914, grandson of Lord Tredegar, Tory, churchman, horseman, landowner, and the last squire of Ystrad House

173   Abertridwr's eligible young men, *c.*1900. Among them is Owen Gibby, carpenter (*back, left*) and John Howells, blacksmith (*back, right*)

174 Dr T. W. Thomas's characteristic cigarette was not forgotten in this portrait presented to him by public subscription in 1929 after he had completed 40 years as a general practitioner in Caerphilly

175 Senghenydd and Aber Valley Co-operative Society committee when their new premises were opened in Senghenydd in the early 1900s. The manager, B. M. Williams, is standing in the centre

176 Llanbradach War Memorial Committee with chairman J. Bassett (*seated, centre*), 1925

177 William Harris, the only man to get out alive after the explosion on 24 May, 1901, which killed 81 colleagues at the Universal Colliery

178 Mrs Ann Jones, who died in 1912, aged 78, one of Abertridwr's monoglot Welsh-speakers, though she spent some time in America as a young woman

179 Businessmen of the 1920s. *Back row:* Jim Davies, groce Owen Jones, printer, Ernest Gray, company secretary; *from* Marcus Harding, builder, Charles Goodfellow, solicitor, an unidentified man

180 Daniel Davies (*right*) lived in a cottage on Caerphilly Mountain and operated Watford Colliery early this century. Its levels still lie below Watford Road, near the chapel. The other man was probably a neighbour

181 William Harris and his wife, of the Garwa Farm, Caerphilly Mountain, and old Mrs Harris, of the *Black Cock Inn, c.*1896

183 (*Opposite*) King Edward VII's visit to Caerphilly in 1907 was organised by this committee

182 Caerphilly Prisoners of War Fund Committee 1916-19. Claude Road and Denscombe are named after its secretary, Claude Denscombe, seated fifth from left, next to the chairman, H. W. Jenkins and treasurer, T. L. Watkins

184 British Legion women at Caerphilly Centotaph, *c.*1928, led by their president, Mrs Capt. Evans (*extreme left*). Third from left is Mrs Gwen Trew, then secretary, now president

The Castle

185 Caerphilly Castle's great gatehouse, c.1900. These and the following pictures show the extent to which the ruins have been restored sinced then

186 The Great Hall was reroofed in 1871 and made available for banquets such as this

187 Jackdaws had a fine home in the ivy-covered Western Gatehouse, 1892

188 The Leaning Tower was always the main attraction, even in 1892

189 The great gatehouse viewed in the 1890s from the spot where the ticket office now stands. It was rebuilt by the Marquess of Bute's men in 1931-33

190 An idyllic view of the castle c.1896 showing meadows where there is now a lake

191/192 Some of the Marquess of Bute's workmen engaged for the restoration of 1928-39

193 The Castle, *c*.1900, showing the old entrance in what is now the lake

194 Work proceeding on the great curtain wall near Cardiff Road, 1935

195 The Great Hall before the banquet given by the Marquess of Bute to the Royal Archaeological Society
in 1871

196 The Leaning Tower dominated the old entrance to the castle

197 'Kissing the Ring', a game for ladies and gentlemen on the Castle Green, 1892

198/199 Caerphilly Cheese stamps. *Top:* The official stamp of Edward Lewis, cheese-taster, lamp-lighter and truancy officer. *Below:* A stamp used by Thomas Rees, 3 Market Street. (Both drawn by W. Lazard, copyright of Glyndwr G. Jones)

ACKNOWLEDGEMENTS

I wish to thank the following for making pictures available:

Mrs Irene Bassett (129, 144, 152, 176, 184); D. J. Baverstock (175); W. A. Beynon (18, 141); Caerphilly District Miners Hospital (159); Caerphilly Library (1, 23, 40, 95-104, 108, 117, 179); Cardiff Central Library (14, 24, 54, 55, 81, 82, 83, 128, 130, 136, 145, 155, 162, 163, 164, 165, 185, 186, 187, 188, 189, 194, 195, 197); Percy Coleman (17, 26, 46, 86, 87, 149); Mr and Mrs J. I. Cordey (51, 52); Lewis Davies (27, 139); Gordon Emmanuel (48, 70); Hubert Gatehouse (5, 118); Mrs B. Gibby (45, 89, 91, 115, 142, 143); John Gittins (21); Ted Harris (180, 181); C. R. Hopkins (36, 127, 154); Mrs Mary Howells (173); Mrs Avril Hurd (44, 47, 60, 61, 126, 151, 168, 170, 171, 174); Mrs Margaret Jenkins (116); Arthur Jones (43, 53); Glyndwr G. Jones (13, 22, 29, 146, 157, 166, 198, 199); H. C. Jones (57); Mrs Knight (10, 11); Llanbradach Workmen's Hall & Institute (172); T. J. McCarthy (72); Mid Glamorgan County Library (6, 7, 9, 19, 160, 161, 190, 193, 196); E. R. Mountford (69, 71, 73-77); National Museum of Wales (134, 135); Mrs Eunice Owen (153); Barrie Owens (37, 50, 124, 138, 140); J. Basil Phillips (20, 67, 114, 132, 133); Frank Piper (33, 35); Mrs C. Pitten (90); Rhymney Valley District Council (2, 3, 4, 78, 131, 156, 183); H. P. Richards (16); Mrs May Richards (59, 88, 178); Mrs Bert Rowland (49); St Martin's Comprehensive School (per R. Parsons) (30, 38, 105, 106, 107, 110-113); H. Simons (122, 123); E. J. Starr (109, 150); Rufus Stephens (31, 32, 39, 84, 85, 92, 93, 94); A. H. Sully (182); David Sutton (137, 148, 158); Ken Thomas (Manchester House) (8, 12, 25, 58, 79, 80, 119, 120, 121, 125); Tonyfelin Chapel (42); Mrs Ann Walters (34, 191, 192); Tudur Watkins (66). The remaining photographs are from the collection of Caerphilly Local History Society.

In addition, Hubert Gatehouse allowed me to reproduce the following copyright pictures taken by him and his late brother, F. W. Gatehouse: (2, 3, 4, 13, 29, 33, 36, 80, 91, 92, 118, 127, 153, 154), and Victor Hardacre gave me permission to use photographs taken by him: (14, 81, 82, 83, 155, 165, 166, 167 194).